Pebble® Plus

Look Inside

Look Inside a Tepee

by Mari Schuh

Consulting Editor: Gail Saunders-Smith, PhD

Consultant: Dr. Troy Johnson, Chair
American Indian Studies
California State University, Long Beach

Capstone
press

Mankato, Minnesota

Pebble Plus is published by Capstone Press,
151 Good Counsel Drive, P.O. Box 669, Mankato, Minnesota 56002.
www.capstonepress.com

1 2 3 4 5 6 14 13 12 11 10 09

Library of Congress Cataloging-in-Publication Data
Schuh, Mari C., 1975–
    Look inside a tepee / by Mari Schuh.
    p. cm. — (Pebble plus. Look inside)
    Includes bibliographical references and index.
    Summary: "Simple text and photographs present tepees, their construction, and their
interaction with the environment" — Provided by publisher.
    ISBN-13: 978-1-4296-2248-6 (hardcover)
    ISBN-10: 1-4296-2248-2 (hardcover)
    1. Tipis — Juvenile literature. 2. Indians of North America — Dwellings — Juvenile literature. I. Title.
E98.D9S34 2009
728 — dc22   2008027653

Editorial Credits
Megan Peterson, editor; Renée T. Doyle, designer; Wanda Winch, photo researcher

Photo Credits
Alamy/Megapress, 9; North Wind Picture Archives/Nancy Carter, 13
iStockphoto/C. L. Kunst, 15; Eric Foltz, 5; Mark Murphy, 24
Nativestock.com/Marilyn Angel Wynn, 7, 21
North Wind Picture Archives/Nancy Carter, 11, 17, 19
Shutterstock/Judy Crawford, 1, 22–23; South12th Photography, back cover, 3; Todd Pierson, front cover

Note to Parents and Teachers

The Look Inside set supports national social studies standards related to people, places, and culture. This book describes and illustrates tepees. The images support early readers in understanding the text. The repetition of words and phrases helps early readers learn new words. This book also introduces early readers to subject-specific vocabulary words, which are defined in the Glossary section. Early readers may need assistance to read some words and to use the Table of Contents, Glossary, Read More, Internet Sites, and Index sections of the book.

Table of Contents

What Is a Tepee?

A tepee is a tent
made of wood poles
and buffalo hides.
The Plains Indians
once lived in tepees.

5

The Plains Indians

moved from place to place

to hunt buffalo.

Tepees were easy

to take down and move.

Building a Tepee

Plains Indian women
built the tepee.
They tied poles together
to form a cone.

Plains Indian women
fit buffalo hides
over the poles.

Logs or stones held the tepee

to the ground.

The tepee door faced east

to greet the morning sun.

Inside a Tepee

The Plains Indians made a fire
in the middle of the tepee.
A hole at the top of the tepee
let out smoke.

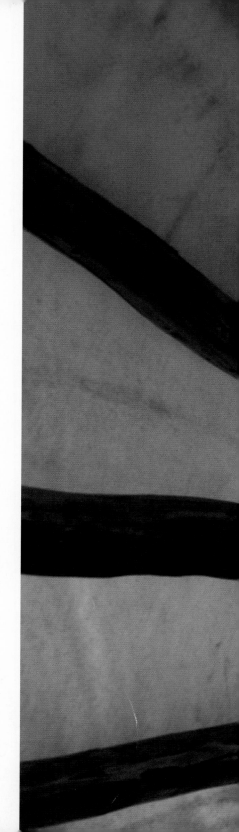

In winter, thick buffalo hides

lined the inside of the tepee.

The hides kept out the wind.

In summer, the bottom

of the tepee was rolled up.

buffalo hide

The Plains Indians slept
under furs and blankets.
Tools and supplies hung
on the tepee's walls.

Tepees Today

Today the Plains Indians

use tepees for ceremonies.

They also use tepees

to learn about the past.

Glossary

buffalo — a large animal with a big, hairy head, a humped back, and short horns, found in North America

ceremony — special actions, words, or music performed to mark an important event

cone — an object or shape with a round base and a point at the top

hide — the skin of an animal; many buffalo hides were sewn together to make a tepee cover; when there were fewer buffalo, tepees were made of strong cloth called canvas.

Plains Indians — Native Americans who lived in the Great Plains of the United States and Canada

Read More

Preszler, June. *Tepees.* Native American Life. Mankato, Minn.: Capstone Press, 2005.

Rau, Dana Meachen. *The Inside Story Tepee.* The Inside Story. New York: Marshall Cavendish Benchmark, 2007.

Internet Sites

FactHound offers a safe, fun way to find educator-approved Internet sites related to this book.

Here's what you do:

1. Visit *www.facthound.com*
2. Choose your grade level.
3. Begin your search.

This book's ID number is 9781429622486.

FactHound will fetch the best sites for you!

Index

Word Count: 163
Grade: 1
Early-Intervention Level: 17